A Primary Teacher's Handbook Art

David Withey

Jane Grosz

Maggie Fulton

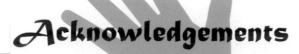
Acknowledgements

David Withey (Senior Adviser), Jane Grosz and Maggie Fulton (advisory teachers) hereby assert their moral rights to be identified as the authors of this work in accordance with the Copyright, Designs and Patents Act 1988.

With thanks to the following schools:
Prescot Primary, Halsnead Primary, Cronton CE Primary, Park View Primary, New Hutte Primary, Roseheath Primary, St Joseph's RC Primary, The Elms, Westvale Primary and St Mary & St Paul's CE Primary.

With thanks also to:
The Walker Art Gallery, Liverpool (for photograph on page 4).

Photographs:
The Bridgeman Art Gallery: 32 and 33 (Hans Holbein, Hans the Younger, Portrait of Henry VIII/Belvoir Castle, Leicestershire); 35 Vanessa Bell, Bathers in a Landscape/Angelica Garnett private collection); 37 (Eugene Manet, Edgar Degar/Christie's, London); 41 (The gold mask, Tutankhamun Treasure c. 1340BC, Egyptian National Museum, Cairo); 58 (Salvador Dali, La Spectre et le Fantome 1912/Christie's, London, © DEMART PRO ARTE BV/DACS 1996); 58 (Monet, Pond with Waterlilies, Musee des Beaux Arts, Caen/Giraudon); 59 (Gustav Klint, Fulfillment/Osterreichische Galerie, Vienna); 59 (Paul Cézanne, Boy in a Red Waistcoat/Buhrle Collection, Zurich).

Ray Young/Georgina Stein (Roehampton Institute London): 10 (bottom); 14; 18 (top and centre); 19 (top and bottom); 23; 24 (two); 49 (bottom right); 56 (top); 60; 63; 64.

Peter and Sandra Mcfall, Gemini Photography, Liverpool: 4; 9; 10 (top and centre); 11 (all three); 13; 15; 16; 17; 20; 21; 22; 25; 26; 27; 28; 29; 30 (all three); 31; 34; 36; 37 (bottom); 38; 40; 41 (child making mask, and the mask); 42 (both); 43 (both); 46 (both); 47 (both); 48; 48 (top right and bottom left); 50; 51 (both); 53 (both); 54 (all five); 56 (centre and bottom); 57; 62.

Catherine Cummings: 12.

Peter Ryan: 61.

Crown copyright is reproduced with the permission of the Controller of HMSO.

| Editor: Catherine Miller | Design: Andy Bailey | Layout artist: Pat Hollingsworth |
| Cover Image: Peter and Sandra McFall, Gemini Photography | | Cover design: Andy Bailey/Alison Colver |

First published 1995 by Folens Limited, Dunstable and Dublin.
Folens Limited, Albert House, Apex Business Centre, Boscombe Road, Dunstable, LU5 4RL, England.

ISBN 1 85276 885-1

Printed in Hong Kong

Contents

Contributors:

Pete Bannister; Chris Hannell; Sue Hopper; Janet Lomax; Jan Martin; Margaret Naylor; Colin Rowling; Meg Sunderam; Trish Walsh.

Additional consultation: Georgina Stein, Roehampton Institute London.

Introduction

The introduction of National Curriculum Art as a foundation subject, in September 1992, established a framework for teaching art across the 5–14 age range.

Coordinators of art in Knowsley Local Education Authority (LEA) primary schools responded to the demands of the document at Key Stage 1 (KS1) and Key Stage 2 (KS2) by collaborating with the advisory service in a borough-wide review of art provision and a reassessment of needs. From that review came the decision to produce a handbook that would help class teachers organise art activities – this book is the culmination of that initiative.

It does not contain prescribed schemes or lessons but provides 'teacher friendly' guidance concerning the requirements of the National Curriculum Art document. It also provides guidance on progression through techniques and areas of experience, resourcing and assessment. It represents considerable commitment by practising teachers and should prove an invaluable planning resource.

This book could not have been produced without the support of the Knowsley LEA, head teachers, teaching colleagues and, most of all, the contributors who gave their own time for no reason other than to enhance the education of children. Folens is proud to be the publishers of a book that reflects the commitment and professionalism of the teaching profession.

Aims of the handbook

To support the teaching of art by:
- Ensuring good practice in art education.
- Providing all the children, regardless of ability, gender or race, with an opportunity to express themselves visually in an enjoyable manner.
- Enabling the children to become visually literate – that is, that they can use and understand art as a form of communication and are able to read and evaluate competently 2D and 3D works of art.
- Developing the children's creative and technical skills so that ideas can be realised and artefacts produced.
- Developing the children's aesthetic sensibilities, enabling them to make informed judgments about art.
- Facilitating the children's design capability.
- Stimulating the children's capacity for imaginative and original thought and experimentation.
- Developing the children's capacity to learn about and observe the world in which they live.
- Encouraging the children's ability to articulate and communicate ideas, opinions and feelings about their own work and that of others.
- Developing the children's ability to value the contribution made by artists, craftworkers and designers and to respond thoughtfully, critically and imaginatively to a variety of ideas, images and objects from many cultures.

Writing a policy statement and scheme of work

The introduction of National Curriculum Art means that schools must produce a 'whole school policy' for art. The difficult task of formulating this policy and scheme of work is usually the responsibility of the Art Coordinator, who may be writing policies for the first time.

Where are we now?
Audit: existing policies, schemes of work, present art and design curriculum, equipment, time allocated to art.

Where do we want to be?
Eg To have a clear and concise scheme of work that is regularly reviewed and flexible; to have a policy that allows for continuity, progression, breadth and balance.

How will be know when we have arrived?
Eg Set a date by which you want the policy in place. Governors and parents will have been involved.

How do we get there?
Eg By collaborating with staff; using support where available (eg advisory service and existing literature), by building on and extending resources by having a planned financial allocation.

A dynamic curriculum
The starting point will always be 'Where are we now?'. When you think you have arrived at where you wanted to be, you ask the question 'Where are we now?' again and so the cyclical process of development continues. When you think there is nowhere else to go you will stand still!

Elements of an art policy and scheme of work

A statement of aims
- What the school wishes to achieve, taking into account multi-cultural issues, equal opportunities and the children's own enthusiasm and enjoyment.

Objectives
- How the school will achieve its aims in relation to the National Curriculum (NC) schemes of work:
  - techniques and processes (relevant to each key stage)
  - lesson examples
  - classroom organisation (eg time resources)
  - learning outcomes (eg skills, knowledge and concepts)
  - differentiation.

Record keeping
- Selected examples, portfolios and reports: NC non-statutory guidance provides some ideas.

Assessment
- Individual and comparative.

Evaluation
- Review and modify.

Resources
- Materials available and required, outside agencies.

Display
- Where, how and when.

Health and safety
- Issues which should be brought to the teacher's attention.

Art in the National Curriculum

	Attainment target 1 *Investigating and Making*	**Attainment target 2** *Knowledge and Understanding*
Key Stage 1	The children should demonstrate that they: • are starting to look closely at the natural and made world and record what they see • are confident in using memory and imagination in developing ideas for art • are willing to explore the use of a variety of materials, tools and resources for practical work • understand that art has its own language, lines, shapes and colours and they can show some awareness of this in their own work • can control tools safely, organise and care for materials and equipment • are developing the practice of planning their work, trying out ideas beforehand and changing it if needed.	The children should demonstrate that they: • can look closely at artefacts and objects, including their own work, and talk about them • have begun to understand that there are connections between their own work and the work of artists, both past and present.
Key Stage 2	The children should demonstrate that they: • can select aspects of the natural and made world and record what they see, imagine and feel • can take some responsibility for gathering information in support of their work and be discriminating in using it • can be selective in their choice and application of materials to suit the task • are developing control, confidence and understanding in using different materials and techniques • can experiment with the elements of art and begin to use formal ways of communicating ideas/feelings • are able to visualise ideas, discuss them and modify them, with justification.	The children should demonstrate that they: • can discuss different purposes of art and describe how artists have represented their ideas, making use of art vocabulary • can recognise and discuss the work of a number of artists, representing different styles and periods, and understand something of the times in which the work was made and how it influenced others • can apply what they have learned from the work of other artists in an imaginative way to inform their own.

Key Stage 1

AT1
Investigating and Making

WHAT IT SAYS (PROGRAMME OF STUDY)	KEY WORDS	WHAT IT MEANS
A Record what has been experienced, observed and imagined.	RECORD	Record responses, including observations of the natural and made environment.
B Recognise images and artefacts as sources of ideas for their work. **C** Select and sort images and artefacts and use this source material as a basis for their work.	RECOGNISE AND SELECT	Gather resources and materials, using them to stimulate and develop ideas.
D Experiment with tools and techniques for drawing, painting, printmaking, collage, and sculpture, exploring a range of materials, including textiles. **E** Experiment with visual elements (eg pattern, texture, colour, line, tone, shape, form and space) to make images and artefacts using a range of media.	EXPLORE	Explore and use 2D and 3D media, experimenting with visual elements to produce their own work.
F Review what they have done and describe what they might change or develop in future work.	REVIEW	Review and modify their work as it progresses.

AT2
Knowledge and Understanding

WHAT IT SAYS (PROGRAMME OF STUDY)	KEY WORDS	WHAT IT MEANS
A Identify, in the school and locality, the work of artists, craftspeople and designers.	IDENTIFY	Identify different types of art produced locally and present them in their own environment.
B Recognise visual elements (eg pattern, texture, colour, line, tone, shape, form, space) both in images and artefacts. **C** Recognise differences and similarities in art, crafts and design from different times and places.	RECOGNISE	Recognise the application of visual elements and the similarity between art, craft and design from different cultures.
D Respond to the ideas, methods or approaches used in different styles and traditions. **E** Describe works of art, craft and design in simple terms and explain what they think or feel about these.	RESPOND AND DESCRIBE	Respond to ideas and methods in the work of other artists and describe them, using simple terms.

The key words have been selected to help teachers understand the Programme of Study.

Key Stage 2

AT1
Investigating and Making

WHAT IT SAYS (PROGRAMME OF STUDY)	KEY WORDS	WHAT IT MEANS
A Develop skills for recording from direct experience and imagination and select and record from first-hand observation.	DEVELOP AND REPRESENT	Record responses, including observations of the natural and made environment.
B Record observations and ideas and collect visual evidence and information using sketchbooks. **C** Experiment with ideas for their work suggested by visual and other source material.	INFLUENCE	Gather resources and materials, using them to stimulate and develop ideas.
D Experiment with and develop control of tools and techniques for drawing, painting, printmaking, collage and sculpture, exploring a range of materials, including textiles. **E** Experiment with and use visual elements to make images and artefacts for different purposes, using a range of media.	EXPERIMENT	Explore and use 2D and 3D media and visual elements, developing control of tools and techniques.
F Reflect on and adapt the children's work in the light of what they intended and consider what they might develop in future work.	EVALUATE	Ensure that the children have fulfilled their original intention and considered future developments.

AT2
Knowledge and Understanding

WHAT IT SAYS (PROGRAMME OF STUDY)	KEY WORDS	WHAT IT MEANS
A Identify, in the school and locality, the materials and methods used by artists, craftspeople and designers.	IDENTIFY AND INVESTIGATE	Develop understanding of materials and methods used by local craftspeople, designers and artists.
B Identify how visual elements (eg pattern, texture, colour, line, tone, shape, form, space) are used in images and artefacts for different purposes. **C** Recognise ways in which works of art, craft and design reflect the time and place in which they are made.	IDENTIFY AND REFLECT	Identify and reflect upon visual elements in art and how art works. Reflect on the time and place in which they are made.
D Compare ideas, methods and approaches used in different styles and traditions. **E** Express ideas and opinions, developing an art/craft/design vocabulary, together with the ability to use knowledge to support views.	COMPARE AND EXPRESS	Compare different ideas and approaches in art across different styles and traditions. Express their ideas using appropriate art vocabulary.

The key words have been selected to help teachers understand the Programme of Study.

A PRIMARY TEACHER'S HANDBOOK – Art

Aspects of a practical art programme

Providing a balance between experience and techniques

An art curriculum needs sufficient continuity so that skills can be developed, refined and internalised and hence become part of an expressive repertoire. To deliver successfully the objectives outlined in the National Curriculum document, schools need to ensure that there is a balance between areas of experience and techniques used.

The areas of experience and techniques outlined in the chart below offer the children a breadth of experience in both 2D and 3D activities.

Each process should be progressive across the two key stages.

	ELEMENTS	PROCESSES	MATERIALS	TECHNIQUES
E X P E R I E N C E	Line	3D work	Clay, dough, Plasticine, papier mâché, card, wood, metal, plastic, wire, tins, rolled newspapers, boxes, tubes, rope, polystyrene, matchsticks, lolly sticks.	Cutting Sewing Glueing
	Tone Colour	Collage	Threads, fibres, fabrics, paper, card, wood, metal, stones, found objects, leather, fur, feathers, grasses, flowers, straws, buttons and glue.	Folding Modelling
	Colour mixing	Drawing	Pencils (B&H), charcoal sticks, wax, crayons, pastels, chalks, brushes and pens (biro, metal nib and fibre).	Colouring Printing
	Patterns	Painting	Brushes (round, flat, foam, soft), sticks, straws, fingers, combs, knives, sponges, scrunched paper etc; paint (powder, ready-mixed and blocks etc).	Rubbing Drawing Engraving
	Texture	Photography	Looking through viewfinders, handling simple cameras, loading and unloading cameras and developing.	Building Assembling
	Shape Form	Printing	Fingers, hands, blocks, fruit, vegetables, found objects, wallpaper, clay, Plasticine, string, leaves, sponge, monoprints, wood, polystyrene, lino and screen.	Dyeing Weaving
	Space	Textiles	Weaving, stitching, threads, fibres, printed, sprayed, tie-dye, batik and appliqué.	Staining Embellishing

Areas of experience

Colour

Early experience will include sorting, rearranging and enjoying the different qualities of colour. Children should be taught to identify and name both primary (red, yellow, blue) and secondary colours (purple, green, orange).

Opportunity should be given for free colour mixing and the children should be encouraged to see subtlety, both in the colour they create and in their natural and made environments.

As children develop their skills they should be able to mix and match colour, use it to create mood and express feelings. They should also understand the meaning of tone, tint and shade.

For further information see Glossary.

Form

Young children need to feel and manipulate materials and be allowed to create spontaneously their own forms, using both rigid and malleable materials. As they progress they should consider space and the relationship of one object to another.

Form should become a vehicle for self expression, as well as being a way of producing work for a specified outcome.

Texture

An awareness of texture can be created through feeling and looking at different surfaces and materials. The children can build on these observations by recreating surfaces with a variety of textures.

As the children progress, opportunity should be provided for experimenting with texture as decoration in design work and as a form of expression.

Designing

Children play with materials and tools naturally – building and demolishing, sorting and collecting – developing an awareness of the qualities and characteristics of various materials.

However, specific design and drawing skills need to be taught, so that the children modify their work and progress. Opportunities should be provided for logical problem solving using more advanced techniques.

In both key stages design work should take place individually and in groups.

Drawing

Children should be encouraged from an early age to explore mark-making with a variety of tools, until they begin to represent images that they observe, remember and imagine.

Awareness of the natural and made environment should be fostered through observation of shape, line, pattern, form and texture, together with experience in drawing and discussion. Children will then develop skills and begin to apply their knowledge and experience of different materials to represent ideas.

Pattern

Pattern is a part of the environment and young children delight in searching for it, then producing their own repeated images using simple shapes. As they progress throughout the key stages they need to experience and experiment, first by overlapping and then with more complex patterns and techniques.

Wallpaper, fabric and the natural environment all offer the children the stimuli to create their own patterns using a variety of methods and media.

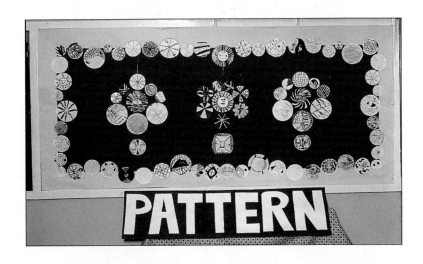

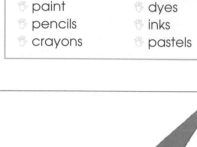

Progression through areas of experience

Extends colour range and hue.

Sorts, selects and describes collections of colour (eg hot and cold).

Names and uses primary colours.

Experiences mixing.

Nursery/Reception

Develops an awareness of diverse colour range in the natural environment.

Develops an awareness of colour in artefacts and design.

Uses colour to express, describe and discuss.

Experiments with colour. Controls colour, hue, tone, shade and creates mood. Applies colour for purpose.

Expresses through colour.

Year 6

Colour

- 🖐 paint
- 🖐 pencils
- 🖐 crayons
- 🖐 dyes
- 🖐 inks
- 🖐 pastels

A PRIMARY TEACHER'S HANDBOOK – *Art*

Form

 3D
 relief

Construction reflects personal ideas.

Becomes aware of natural and made forms and their environments.

Uses tools to produce forms.

Handles, feels and manipulates materials.

Constructs, builds, destroys.

Nursery/Reception

Experiences modelling.

Expresses ideas and feelings using different methods and media.

Understands the qualities and suitability of materials for specific purposes.

Extends techniques, using a wider variety of materials.

Develops more complex methods of construction.

Investigates, analyses and interprets natural and made forms and environments.

Considers light, shadow, form and space.

Year 6

A PRIMARY TEACHER'S HANDBOOK – *Art*

Texture

 collage   wood
thread   fibres
clay   metal
plastic   stone

Has a sensory experience, manipulates materials.

Develops an awareness of texture, different surfaces and qualities.

Nursery/Reception

Makes rubbings.

Produces collage using different textures.

Uses materials to develop relief patterns and pictures.

Is aware of the properties of materials and surfaces.

Looks at and discusses decoration in different forms and cultures.

Makes use of made and natural textures in design and expressive work.

Year 6

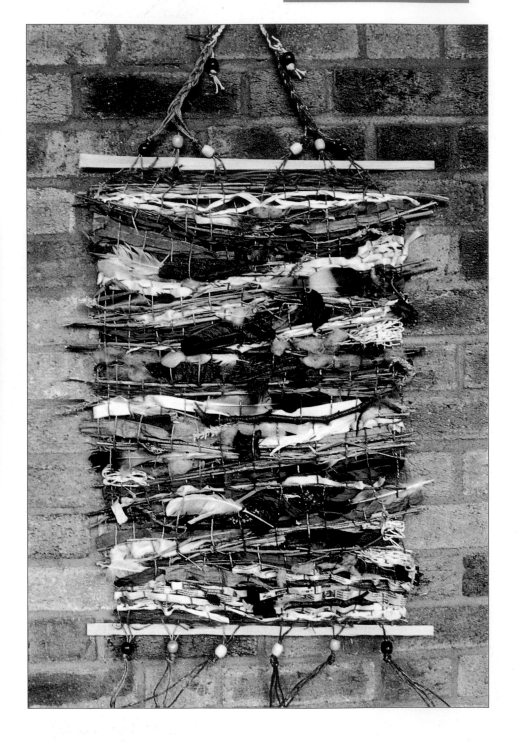

Designing

- 2D and 3D
- spontaneous
- planned

Plays with materials and tools.

Builds and demolishes, sorts, collects and discusses.

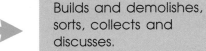

Nursery/Reception

Explores all areas of experience.

Develops an awareness of tools and materials, characteristics and qualities.

Uses skills for specific purposes.

Solves problems, communicates ideas through talking and drawing.

Works out new ideas, reviewing and modifying where necessary.

Makes things spontaneously, discussing possibilities and uses.

Applies knowledge to solve problems using more advanced techniques.

Uses logical and intuitive ways of working.

Takes part in problem-solving, in groups or individually. Experiments with processes.

Year 6

Drawing

- pencils
- pens
- fingers
- chalks
- brushes
- charcoal

Has experience of a variety of tools, eg fingers, chalks, pencils, pens and brushes.

Experiments with a variety of tools, materials and surfaces.

Nursery/Reception

Explores ways of representing what they observe, remember and imagine.

Develops an awareness of the natural and made environments through drawing and discussion.

Investigates and communicates ideas and feelings.

Studies the qualities of shape, line, pattern, form, texture, colour, tone, tints and shade in the environment.

Experiments with techniques and mediums to produce different effects.

Applies knowledge and experience of different materials to represent ideas.

Shows an awareness of dark, light, shape, form, pattern and texture.

Develops fantasy and imagination through drawing.

Year 6

Produces designs using drawings.

Pattern

🖐 printed	🖐 embossed
🖐 dyed	🖐 rubbed
🖐 painted	🖐 imprinted

Repeats shape and form through painting, drawing and basic printing.

Is aware of and has experience of simple pattern-making.

Nursery/Reception

Is aware of relief patterns and has experience of rubbings.

Arranges made and natural items into patterns.

Has experience of repeating and overlapping patterns.

Experiments with a variety of formal and informal patterns.

Looks at more complex patterns and discusses them.

Analyses and records patterns using different methods, using the environment as a stimulus.

Designs and makes a pattern, applying knowledge.

Makes patterns expressing mood.

Makes pattern for a specific purpose, eg wallpaper or fabric book cover.

Year 6

Drawing

As with 'Areas of experience'.

Painting

Spontaneous painting is the key to early art development. Very young children enjoy exploring mark-making and creating images using different papers and tools.

At the same time the children should be introduced to colour mixing and shown the different effects achieved by various brush sizes.

The children should be exposed to a variety of artwork, both original and reproduced, and given the opportunity to paint from observation and from imagination.

As they develop, they should begin to be able to plan outcomes and select appropriate materials and tools.

3D work

As with other areas of experience the children will explore and manipulate 3D materials naturally. They should be given a wide range of malleable and rigid items with which to experiment.

As they progress they become aware of form, space, texture, pattern, weight, balance and the properties of materials.

A wide variety of tools, adhesives and ways of fixing should be made available so that they can develop their own responses through observation and experimentation. (For specific information on pottery see pages 54–57.)

After the early stages of sorting, cutting and stitching materials have been experienced, more complex activities can be introduced. For instance, sewing with a variety of objects (buttons and so on) and sticking with a variety of adhesives.

Collage

Collage has close links with texture and textile work.

Printmaking

Printmaking offers a wonderful experience for children of all ages. Each creation in printmaking is always a success, regardless of the children's motor control or drawing ability. They can produce several prints from one block, on a variety of coloured papers, or with coloured inks.

At KS1 the children begin by exploring random prints made using simple objects, progressing to a range of printmaking activities, using materials such as clay, polystyrene, collage and string.

At KS2 the children build on previous knowledge to produce images that represent the natural world and recreate pattern and texture.

Creating an image involving texture can be an enjoyable experience, with the children being able to talk about their work and problem-solve.

Aspects of symmetry and informal balance, together with an awareness of positive and negative shapes, can be introduced at a later stage.

Textiles

The techniques used here are similar to those needed for collage and texture. Young children love to explore different materials and as they become familiar with them they should be taught skills in simple weaving and stitching.

The children can begin to create interesting designs and patterns using stitching, weaving and printing, including specialised techniques such as batik screen printing and tie-dye.

The children's knowledge of the textiles of other countries and genres can be used as a stimulus, together with observations and analysis of natural objects such as bark and foliage.

Photography

Early experience of photography will include looking at photographic images, discussing things such as colour, scale, movement, mood and feelings.

The children should be made aware of cameras, mirrors, lenses, photobooths and binoculars and should be encouraged to gain hands-on experience of these.

At a more advanced stage, the alteration or manipulation of images can be attempted and simple slides created using readily available school materials. Photograms and pin-hole photography offer opportunities for the children to experiment and explore basic photography in an imaginative and creative way.

Once the children understand the basic methods of creating images, they will be able to develop the ability to plan outcomes, using the right procedures and materials to realise their ideas.

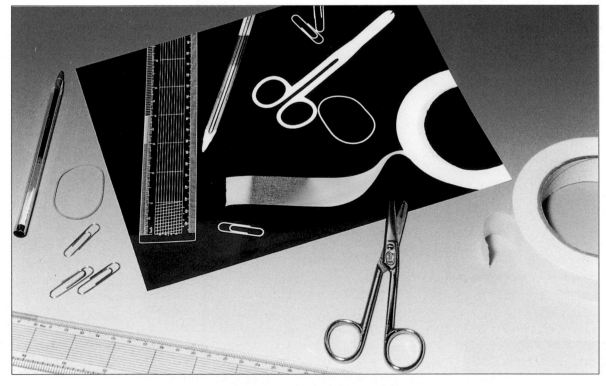

Progression through techniques

Drawing

Nursery/Reception

Enjoys making marks, signs and symbols on a variety of types of paper. (Early drawing is akin to babbling in speech.)

Is spontaneously expressive, using linear marks, curves and lines.

- Uses line to represent objects such as still life/environment.
- Uses line to represent something remembered.
- Uses line to represent an imaginary subject.

Explores tone using different grades of pencil, pastel, chalk.

- Uses line and tone to represent objects such as still life/environment.
- Uses line and tone to represent something remembered.
- Uses line and tone to represent imaginary objects.

Explores shading, using different media.

Draws familiar thing from different viewpoints, using a variety of scales.

Uses a limited range of materials to produce lines, tones and shades.

Is happy experimenting with line, tone and shade.

- Uses line, tone and shade to represent something observed.
- Uses line, tone and shade to represent something remembered.
- Uses line, tone and shade to represent something imagined.

Uses appropriate media and techniques for a specific outcome.

Year 6

Painting

Explores mark-making using thick brushes, foam and sponge brushes. Experiments with and enjoys colour.

Explores making marks on a variety of papers.  Uses a variety of tools to spread paint. For instance, straws, matchsticks.

Creates patterns using different tools and colours.

Nursery/Reception

Uses colour and marks to express mood.

Represents something observed, remembered or imagined, using colour/tools.

Introduces different types of brushes for specific purposes.

Uses techniques, colours, tools and effects to represent something observed, remembered or imagined. Investigates symbols, shapes, form and composition. Explores the effect on paint of adding water, glue, sand, sawdust, etc.

Uses different methods, colour and a variety of tools/techniques to express mood.

Explores the effect of light and colour, texture and tone on natural and made objects.

Creates different effects by using a variety of tools and techniques such as dots, scratches and splashes. 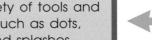 Introduces primary and secondary colours with the addition of black and white and other hues.

Year 6

3D work

Nursery/Reception

Handles, feels and manipulates rigid and malleable materials.

 Pulls apart and reconstructs basic shapes.

 Becomes aware of form, feel, texture, pattern and weight.

 Experiments with basic tools on rigid and plastic materials.

Compares and recreates form and shape to natural and made environments.

 Creates texture using rigid and plastic materials and a variety of tools.

Looks at 3D work from a variety of genres and cultures and develops own response through experimentation.

 Uses stimuli to create simple 2D and 3D images using a variety of tools and materials.

 Recreates images in 2D and 3D, looking at one area of experience, eg recreate a landscape picture, focusing on texture.

 Explores how stimuli can be used as a starting point for 3D work with a particular focus on form, shape, pattern, texture and colour.

 Recreates 2D images in a 3D piece (eg a dragon in a story, the house of the 'three little pigs').

 Makes imaginative use of the knowledge they have acquired of tools, techniques and materials to express own ideas and feelings.

 Begins to look at colour and pattern in 3D structures, transferring the knowledge to their own work.

 Shows an awareness of texture, form and shape by recreating an image in 3D form.

Year 6

A PRIMARY TEACHER'S HANDBOOK – *Art*

© Folens

Collage

Nursery/Reception

 → Handles different materials from a class 'bit box'. → Selects and sorts, cuts, tears, stitches and discusses.

Sorts according to specific qualities, eg warm, cold, rough, smooth, shiny and dull.

Engages in more complex activities, eg cutting and sewing a variety of materials to include forms.

Has experience of adhesives and decides on the most effective for a given task.

Develops experience in embellishing, using more advanced stitching and appliqué techniques like those used in embroidery.

Develops skills of overlapping and overlaying.

Applies knowledge of different techniques as a form of expression.

Embellishes, using a variety of techniques, including drawing, painting and printing.

Develops awareness of contrasts in textures and colours.

Selects and uses materials to achieve a specific outcome.

Designs an artefact, using knowledge of techniques, for a specified outcome.

Experiments with creating mood, feeling, movement and areas of interest.

Uses the natural environment and/or townscapes to stimulate collage work.

 Interprets stories, poems, music and other stimuli.

Year 6

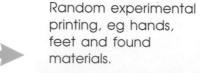**Printmaking**

Random experimental printing, eg hands, feet and found materials.

Uses one colour of paint or ink on a block to explore random images.

Nursery/Reception

Year 6

Experiments with approaches used by other artists, making imaginative use of them.

Carries out screen printing.

Builds up a collage background or a painting through printmaking.

Designs prints for fabrics, book covers and wallpaper.

Recreates a scene observed, remembered or imagined, through collage printing.

Builds up drawings and images of whole or parts of items using various printmaking techniques, eg polystyrene, string, card shapes and relief.

Recreates images through relief printing, using card.

A PRIMARY TEACHER'S HANDBOOK – *Art*

© Folens

Repeating patterns, random or organised, on a variety of papers and with a range of blocks.

 Extends repeated patterns – overlapping shapes using two contrasting colours, eg red and yellow, building up printed patterns.

Explores and recreates patterns and texture with an extended range of materials, eg sponges, leaves, fruit, netting, wood, creased foil, clay and Plasticine.

Explores images through mono-printing on a variety of papers.

Explores images and recreates patterns and texture using wallpaper, polystyrene and string, printing on a variety of papers.

Explores colour mixing through printing, using two colours and a variety of materials.

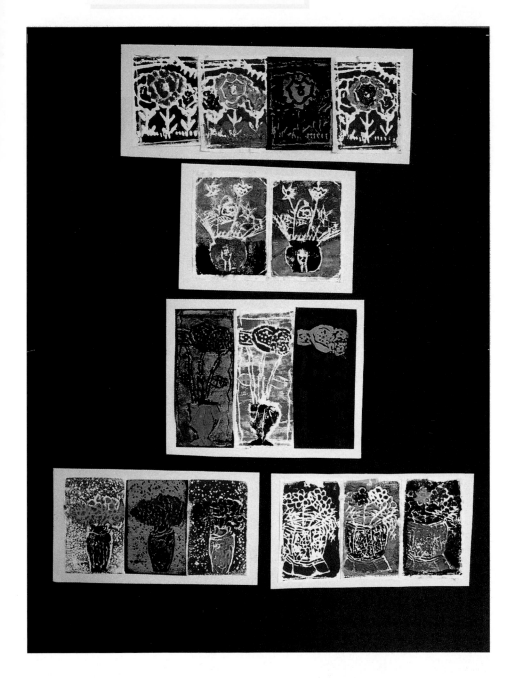

Makes connections between own work and patterns in the local environment and at home, eg curtains, wallpapers and book designs.

 Compares own image and pattern making with that of a well-known artist, such as William Morris.

 Uses printing to represent the natural environment.

Photography

Becomes aware of photography as an art form.

Collects photographs for a theme.

Nursery/Reception →

Year 6

Is aware of all the basic principles and processes of photography, together with its limitations.

Superimposes, using a combination of techniques and photographs.

Uses a pin-hole camera to explore close-up images, distant images, ghost images and movement.

Builds a pin-hole camera.

Creates visions and images by exploring the use of materials on photographic paper which is exposed to light, eg leaves and building blocks.

Explores negative and positive.

Creates simple images on photographic paper by placing shapes and materials on paper and fixing in chemicals.

A PRIMARY TEACHER'S HANDBOOK – *Art* © Folens

Is aware that there are famous or specialist photographers.

 • Develops an awareness of scale, perspective, movement and colour in photography.
• Develops an awareness of mood, emotions and feelings in photography.

Alters images through jigsaws, collage, positive and negative shapes.

Has experience of a variety of lenses, such as cameras, telescopes and binoculars.

Is aware of the uses of lenses and their effects on images.

Experiences the effect of light and magnification on transparencies.

Explores creative slide-making using felt pens, feathers, gauze and food dyes.

Colour and positioning of the strips have been used here to give an impression of depth.

Understands that videos and camcorders are forms of photography and the principle of how they work.

 Makes a flick book to create the impression of movement.

 Is aware of the processes by which photographs and slides are developed.

Textiles

Nursery/Reception

→ Handles, feels and manipulates materials such as threads, cottons, woods, raffia and grass.

→ Is aware of colour, texture and shape.

Sorts, collects, discusses and pulls apart cloth and threads.

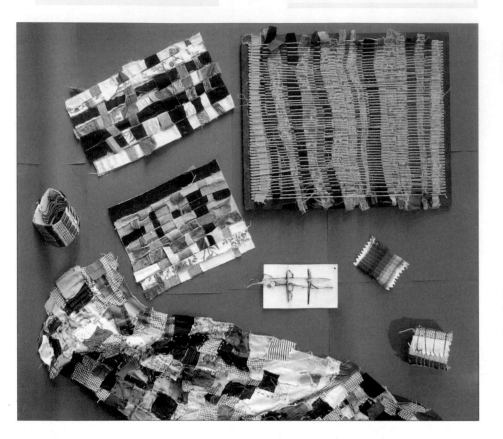

Stitches threads and fibres; cuts threads and fibres (can be linked to collage work).

Simple weaving with strong wool through a stiff card loom.

Weaves paper, progressing from one to two colours.

Able to discriminate between materials.

Prints on fabrics.

Cuts and stitches patterns.

← Stitching – uses various needles to produce more complex patterns.

Experiments with soft sculpture; cuts and joins patterns, embellishing the components.

Uses plaiting, pinning, stapling, stitching and sewing techniques.

Simple stitching: uses a large needle to make straight stitches.

Designs shapes, tie-dyes, makes prints and batik for a specific outcome.

Develops an awareness of the natural environment through colour matching.

Year 6

Dyes fabrics using techniques such as tie-dye and batik.

← Uses contrasting colours in stitching and weaving.

Incorporating attainment targets into an art scheme

AT1 Investigating and Making

In both Key Stage 1 and Key Stage 2 the children need to develop skills in forming ideas from observations. They do this by using their sketchbooks, working from direct experience, memory and imagination, and by utilising a wide variety of reference materials.

Drawing, painting and 3D work are all ways in which ideas and feelings can be expressed. The children need to be provided with opportunities to explore a wide range of tools and materials.

By investigating them and building on previous knowledge, the children will develop an understanding of which tools and materials are best used for specific tasks.

In Key Stage 2 it is expected that the children will be able to decide on the types of materials and methods investigated in Key Stage 1 which are most suited to producing a more recognisable representation.

Observing

Observational work develops a discerning eye for detail, opportunities for greater familiarity with objects in the local area and enables children to build up a visual memory of what things look like.

Introduce children to observational drawings and paintings by relating them to the children's areas of interest. They will then start to appreciate the possibilities of controlling and directing marks.

The children should base their work more and more on their own observations, so that by the end of Key Stage 2 they are experienced in using sketchbooks and notebooks.

The accent should be on enabling the children to appreciate and understand the structure of the natural and made world, by discussing and describing their ideas and feelings.

Memory and imagination

Each statement in Key Stage 2 builds on a related one in Key Stage 1. For example, in Key Stage 1 the children are asked to record images from direct observation, memory and imagination. In Key Stage 2 they are asked to select, analyse and record images from direct observation, memory and imagination, using a variety of materials and methods.

When children do not have something in front of them to observe directly, they need to be stimulated in other ways, for example by:
– works of fiction, poetry and the children's own work
– music
– historical and geographical materials
– collections of objects from visits
– folklore
– festivals.

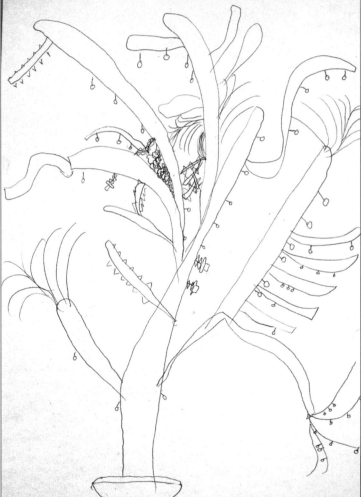

Expressive work

This is different from imaginative work, in that the children are expected to show not just *what* the object or subject looked like but *how* they felt about it.

All kinds of things make us feel happy or sad, threatened or joyful, and children can find ways of expressing feelings through markings, drawings and paintings, or through 3D work involving colour, texture, line and form.

AT2 Knowledge and Understanding

'Knowledge and Understanding' of art is traditionally an unfamiliar aspect of the art curriculum to most primary school teachers.

The children's own art is enriched when they are exposed to the work of a wide range of other artists, craftworkers and designers. They become aware of the influence and impact that art and design have upon everyday life and this knowledge will help them to understand art and its purpose in a wider context.

At Key Stage 1 the children need to be aware that there are a number of different types of art and of how art has changed through history, so distinguishing between the past and present. The children should be given the opportunity to compare their own artwork with others' on a similar theme or subject and make simple connections between the two.

As they progress through Key Stage 2 the children need to compare different kinds of art and design and discuss, in practical terms, how a particular piece was made. In addition, they need to understand each artist's reasons for producing the work – for instance, one reason may be patronage.

Teachers need to ensure that children are exposed to a balance of artwork in a variety of styles from different periods and traditions.

Discussion needs to take account of how art has developed and how it has been influenced by particular artists or groups of artists. Practical experimentation will be stimulated by such discussion and the children should be encouraged to develop their own skills by exploring the methods and approaches that

are used by other artists.

While progressing through the key stages the children will begin to recognise that art and design is not just 'something you do in school' but forms an integral part of everyday life in all communities and cultures. By

identifying, understanding and making imaginative use of their own work and that of other artists and designers, cross-curricular links can be developed, with particular reference to history, technology, PSE, drama and English.

Teachers and pupils should look at:	artworks such as: paintings, sculptures, prints, slides, illustrations, posters, books, collected items.
Children should:	look, describe, speculate, investigate, discuss, compare.
And consider:	shape, texture, colour, pattern, line, tone, mood/atmosphere, composition.

AT2
Studying works of art

FIGURATIVE – example using the portrait of Henry VIII.

Key Stage 1

Content

- What are we looking at?
- What is in the picture?
- What is the man wearing?
- Is he dressed in clothes of today?
- What is he doing?
- Is he big or small?
- Does he look real?
- How is he standing?
- Do you think he is rich or poor?
- Do you think he is Important?
- Why, or why not?
- What sort of a house do you think he lived in?
- Do you think the artist liked the man in the picture?
- Do you think he looks happy, sad, frightened or angry?
- What is he holding?
- Can you tell anything about how Henry is feeling?

Form

- What colours have been used?
- Why do you think the artist used these colours?
- Can you see any patterns?
- Can you see any light or dark parts?

Process

- What is the picture made of?
- Do you think the artist used sketches, or photographs, or something else?

Key Stage 2

Content

- Who is in the picture?
- Look at Henry's facial expression, his pose and his gesture.
- Do you think he looks powerful?
- What can you tell about Henry from the portrait?
- Do you think the figure is in proportion?
- Why do you think it is painted in these proportions?
- Why do you think Henry wanted his picture painted?
- What sort of image is the artist trying to portray?
- What is a portrait commission?

Form

- Discuss the colours and patterns used.
- From which direction is the light coming?
- Which part of the picture draws your attention?
- How has the artist done this?

Process

- What sort of paint do you think has been used?
- How do you think the paint has been applied?
- How long do you think it took to paint it?
- Do you think Henry stood there all the time?
- Do you think the artist drew a picture of it before he painted it?
- What do you think the sitter did with it?
- Who do you think paid for it?
- What relationship do you think the artist had with the sitter?
- What mood or feeling is created by the colours used?

These questions may be used as starting points for class discussions and can be adapted for different works of art.

AT2
Studying works of art

ABSTRACT – it isn't necessary that all of the following questions are asked each time the children are presented with a work of art, but it is important that some from each category are used.

Key Stage 1 and Key Stage 2

Content

- What are we looking at?
- What is in the picture?
- Do you think the artist looked at a subject or used memory or imagination?
- What do you think the work is about?
- What can you see in this work?
- Why do you think the artist created this image?

Form

- How has the artist used space?
- Is there a main shape or a combination of shapes?
- What colours can you see?
- Are there any patterns?
- Has the artist used line or tone in the work?
- Are there any dark parts, light parts and so on?
- Do the colours work, do they blend or do they contrast?
- Is there one main colour or several?
- Does the work have a texture?

Process

- How was the work made?
- What materials were used?
- How do you think the artist started this work? Which part came first and which last?
- Do you think the artist used sketches, photographs or something else?
- How long do you think it took to make – a short time or a long time?
- What skills has the artist used?
- What knowledge did he or she apply?

Mood

- Is there a mood or a feeling about the piece?
- Can you associate any smells or sounds with the work?
- Is there any life or feeling of life and nature in the work?
- What do you think the artist was feeling during the making of the work?
- Is it quiet, noisy, happy, sad, frightened or calm?
- Does it remind you of anything?
- How does the work make you feel?

A PRIMARY TEACHER'S HANDBOOK – *Art*

Bathers in a landscape *by Vanessa Bell, with
a child's interpretation of the work, far left.*

Combining 'Investigating and Making' with 'Knowledge and Understanding'

Asking questions

Encourage the children to observe pictures then ask the following questions:

- What has the artist left out and why?
- What has been added?
- What sort of light do you think was used?
- Has realistic colouring been used?
- Has the subject been simplified?
- Which direction did the light come from?
- Did the subject remain static throughout?

Works of art are usually inspired by something the artist has seen or experienced. In the case of a painter, It has necessitated the translation of something 3D into something 2D.

To help a child understand and really look at a painting, it is sometimes useful to suggest they reconstruct the painting in a 3D form.

All such reconstructions help the children become aware of how artists work; they are also able to make comparisons between the artists' response and their own to the same subject matter.

Once the children have considered the questions above, they can be asked to produce their own work from similar source materials. Ask them to discuss the selections and choices they have made.

Activities

In order to help the children look at a painting and understand it, ask them to:

- describe the painting and write about it
- reconstruct the scene by dressing and posing as characters from the picture
- make studies of textures and patterns within the work
- enlarge and reproduce small portions of the work, using a viewfinder
- reconstruct a still life work, using similar materials
- create an image in the style of the artist.

Classroom practice

It is essential to plan an art activity if effective learning is to take place. The following points may prove useful for teachers to ask themselves when structuring activities.

Planning an art programme

- Is work to be individual or group based?
- Is teacher expertise involved?
- How much teacher input is required?
- Are materials available?
- Is the work isolated or cross-curricular?
- Does the activity match the children's ability?
- Is there a variety of media and tools with which the children can explore and experiment?

- Are there opportunities to look at and talk about a variety of artists' and designers' work?
- Are the children being given enough opportunities to make imaginative use of their own work and that of other artists?
- Has allowance been made for the differing times of completion of work by individuals?
- Will the children's art vocabulary be extended?

- Has time been allowed for the children to evaluate their own and others' work?
- Are the children being encouraged to develop as individuals rather than conform to the pre-conceived ideas and values of others?
- Will the activity extend the children's creative skills, observation, memory and imagination?

Collaboration between art and other curriculum areas

Here is an example of how a cross-curricular topic, 'The Family', could be stimulated by works of art.

The Family

The circular diagram radiates outward from the centre "THE FAMILY" through concentric rings:

Centre: THE FAMILY

Ring – AIMS AND OBJECTIVES OF TOPIC

Ring – REVIEW OTHER STIMULUS – PAINTINGS SUCH AS:
- Degas – The Belliili family 1859.
- Gauguin – The painter's family in the garden 1880.
- David Hockney – My parents 1975-1977.

DISCUSS – Works of art
- Puoli's family tree.
- Past generations. Family trees.

DISCUSS – MEMORY / EXPERIENCE
- Family memorabilia.
- Photographs.

DISCUSS – Recreate family group by dressing and posing children.

DISCUSS – Write about and discuss how the family might be feeling in a given work of art.

MODIFY – OBSERVATIONS
- Drawings of own family members and other families.

MODIFY – Talk about family occasions. Weddings. celebrations.

MODIFY – Look at media representation of families; for example, films, books, advertising.

MODIFY – Look at and resolve family conflicts through role play, puppets and so on.

MODIFY – Write and perform a play about a family occasion for a variety of audiences.

EVALUATE – Discuss different aspects of family in different cultures, past and present.

EVALUATE – Study families in different cultures worldwide.

EVALUATE – IMAGINATION
- Poems
- Stories
- Accounts of family occasions and relationships.

REVIEW – Discuss and write about families, eg. changing roles, nuclear and extended families.

REVIEW – Explore historical elements of family life in a variety of cultures.

REVIEW – Made large representations of family groups using different media.

DISCUSS – Develop their own 2D and 3D work in a variety of media and talk about it.

Assessment

Originality and creativity are difficult to define and can be interpreted in many different ways. Nevertheless, it is important to find ways of assessing the extent of pupils' achievements, as the results can prove useful, providing information about:

- how successful the teaching and planning programme has been
- how well the children are developing
- what is needed in future planning.

Each activity needs clear aims and objectives relevant to the child's stage of development and, while assessing, it is important that personal circumstances and environment are taken into consideration.

When assessing the success of this planning for development, the children's work should be compared to that of other children of the same age, not to adult art and ability. Discussion with the children should reveal how and why the work has been brought about and the extent of his or her understanding.

In addition, assessment should not take place in isolation, but should be part of a continuous teaching and learning process which is based on work produced throughout the year. A natural form of evaluation and assessment will occur during the process of each lesson.

The children's ability to be both critical and appreciative of art will be developed by sharing

Children should be encouraged to discuss their work with their teacher and parents.

views and opinions. They should be encouraged to justify intentions and give reasons for their interpretation of the task. It should then be possible to assess whether or not the criteria have been fulfilled for a particular lesson and if the children have made full use of different stimuli, techniques and media by building upon previous experiences.

A simple response to a task would focus on the content of the work done and use of materials and techniques rather than interpretation.

As responses develop, qualities such as colour, texture, form and composition would also be taken into consideration and, in addition, moods, feelings, attitudes and personal preferences would be referred to and discussed.

A more sophisticated response would be influenced by period and culture, together with

exposure to other artists' and designers' work.

While assessing skills, knowledge and understanding should be an integral part of the process.

Recording and reporting on the children's progress in art

In order to assess the children's progress, it might be useful to ask the following general questions:

- Are sketchbooks passed on throughout key stages?
- Is a selection of the children's artwork retained?
- Are individual assessment records kept?
- Are records passed on from year to year?
- Is information passed on at the end of each key stage?

Suggested criteria for assessment

Criteria for assessment need to be agreed by the whole staff and be incorporated in the school policy document.

Possible criteria are:
- Use of colour, if used.
- How sensitively, and with what variety, the medium has been used.
- How texture is represented.
- How space and form are used.
- Selection of view.
- Position of work on paper.
- Use of light.
- Use of tone.
- Skills of observation and recording.
- Capability with tools.
- Appropriateness of medium.
- Quality of imagination.
- Inventiveness and ideas.
- Ability to review and appraise work.
- Ability to make connections between own work and that of other artists.
- Pleasure.
- Enthusiasm.
- Interest and motivation.
- Contribution to discussion.
- Competence in activities.
- Ability to produce both 2D and 3D work.
- Understanding and appreciation of artworks.
- Use of art vocabulary.
- Developing self-critical skills.
- Originality.

National Curriculum Art	
Child _____	
Teacher _____ Year Group _____	
_____ Date _____	
ACTIVITY – Make a death mask based on observation of Tutankhamun	
How well did I do?	**Child/teacher comment**
Use of colour	
Skills of observation	
Capability with tools	
Making connections between own work and Egyptian artwork	
Pleasure	
Enthusiasm	

Each activity should be planned with specific criteria in mind. Photographs of the child's work can be placed in the child's portfolio as a record of achievement.

Characteristics of children's work

The following are guidelines of what characterises children's work at various stages. It must be remembered that the children's individual stages of development and experiences should be considered.

Reception to Year 1

At this stage the children should be able to:

- draw and paint symbolically, features may be missing from faces and houses and trees may all be of a standard shape
- use mostly primary colours unless directed otherwise
- use a random selection of tools (eg brushes, sponges, pencils, pastels)
- represent people as being larger than houses or other buildings
- mix colours
- begin to handle correctly simple tools (eg scissors, glue spreaders and clay tools)
- represent observed objects differently to how they appear (eg purple leaves)
- create simple images from both malleable and rigid materials
- be independent in thoughts and ideas for images
- discriminate between simple materials according to their qualities (eg rough, smooth, hard, soft, bright and dull)
- be original and inventive and talk about their work
- make simple connections between their work and that of others.

Year 2

At this stage the children should be able to:

- include more details in paintings and drawings (eg ears, fingers and toes)
- develop a knowledge of simple secondary colours (eg orange, brown, green, purple)
- choose from a limited selection of tools for a given task
- represent figures in more realistic proportions
- look closely at details when observing and recording and depict them accurately
- show inventiveness and originality with both malleable and rigid materials
- explain clearly what they set out to achieve
- make connections between their own work and that of other artists, scriptwriters and designers.

Years 3 and 4

At this stage the children should be able to:
- draw and paint, paying closer attention to proportion and detail (eg clothes and hair)
- differentiate between colours and patterns and exhibit a knowledge of secondary colours
- mix hues of one colour
- be more selective in their choice of tools
- begin to show aspects of 3D work
- use media sensitively and with variety
- position work more selectively on paper
- represent light and dark
- create a depth of tone
- portray observations accurately and sensitively
- extend their imagination
- be independent and inventive
- review and change work if necessary to develop ideas
- show a development of knowledge of other artists, craftworkers and designers
- make imaginative use of this knowledge.

Years 5 and 6

At this stage the children should be able to:
- pay attention to finer details (eg how hair grows, overlapping and movement in pictures)
- include details (eg patterns on bags, badges, jewellery and facial expressions)
- display more 3D qualities in their work
- use colour more appropriately
- use light and dark effectively
- create different depths of tone through shading
- extend different depths of tone through shading
- extend their knowledge of the work of other artists, to enhance their own imagination and inventiveness.

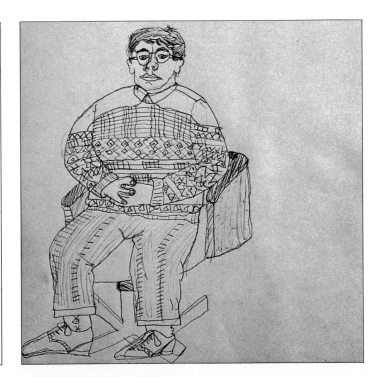

Summative assessment in art

Name	Age	Class

AT1 – Investigating and Making

	From observations	From imagination	From memory
Work produced			
2D work	Materials	Tools	Techniques
3D work	Materials	Tools	Techniques
Use of sketchbook Research Ideas Planning Design			

Design work

Areas requiring further development

A PRIMARY TEACHER'S HANDBOOK – *Art*

Summative assessment in art

Name	Age	Class

AT2 – Knowledge and Understanding

Making critical reference to artists' work
(Looking at and talking about work experienced in galleries, on film or slides, in books, using prints and the environment.)

Applying knowledge of the work of other artists to their own work

Reviewing and modifying their own work

Identifying art of different periods and styles

Identifying art of other cultures

Understanding of specific art terms
(eg portrait, space, wash and tone)

Understanding art concepts
(eg Renaissance, Impressionism,
Pop Art, Fauvism, Cubism)

Knowledge and understanding of above applied to own work

The value of display

Why display?

- To provide a visually stimulating environment.
- To arouse curiosity.
- To give purpose and value to the children's work.
- To give confidence and a sense of achievement.
- To develop an aesthetic awareness in the children.
- To provide an opportunity to look at others' work.
- To encourage a positive attitude towards the environment.
- To encourage a higher standard of work.
- To stimulate interest and promote development.

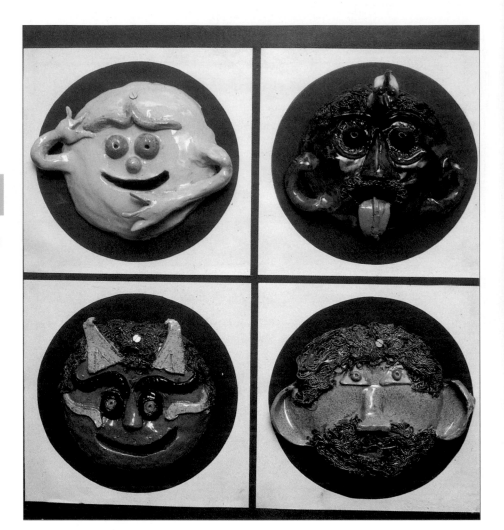

A PRIMARY TEACHER'S HANDBOOK – *Art*

What to display

- The children's works of art (eg paintings, drawings and prints).
- The children's 3D work (eg pottery, papier mâché and mixed media models).
- Works of art – reproductions of paintings from different cultures.
- Photographs.
- Books.
- Posters.
- Original works of art and craft (eg parents' work, teachers' work and work from secondary schools).
- Natural and made objects.

Đow to display

Children learn from everything around them and so display should be seen as a teaching aid. In this context children should be taught to display work effectively and become critical about the appearance of their work space.

Ways in which the teaching environment can be improved:

Background

- The choice of background on which the displays are mounted is important.
- It is a good idea to cover display boards in a variety of ways to create an eye-catching contrast.
- With 3D display, dull colours often form the most effective background and objects on display usually look best when grouped in some way.

Mounting a display

- Cutting lines should be ruled.
- Methods of mounting should be as inconspicuous as possible (sewing pins show less than drawing pins).
- Lettering should be clear and precise.
- Margins should be of an adequate size.
- Cow gum is recommended.
- Blu-Tack or similar is an effective bonding agent.

It is important to make sure that:

- Work is parallel with the top, bottom and sides of mount.
- Both sides of the mount are the same width.
- The top and bottom are either the same width as the sides, or the bottom is slightly wider to include a title and name plate.
- Work can either be single or double mounted. Double is more effective.

Layout of display

- Using a variety of shades in moderation can be effective.
- An overcrowded display loses impact.
- The eye can be drawn to a focal point by using lines.
- A planned sequence is often effective.
- Contrast will often draw the eye to a focal point.

To highlight a display use:

colour   – create contrast using paper and textiles

artificial lighting – spotlight, colour, shadow

natural lighting – for transparent work use windows.

To create additional display space use:

corrugated card   – on walls, on cupboards, free standing

wooden trellis   – on walls or as divider

polystyrene tiles   – on walls or suspended from beams

hessian wallpaper – in a wide range of colours

rush matting   – which can be fixed on to hardboard

folding airer   – with hardboard shelving

boxes   – as an island display, covered in fabric

the ceiling   – hang mobiles from it.

Computers in art

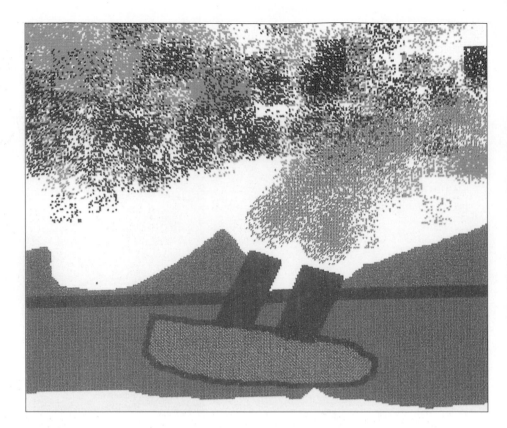

A fast developing technology

Artists have always used new materials and technology to create their vision of reality and express emotions about it. This developmental progression has been reflected within art education too, culminating in today's increasing use of widely available technology, such as the computer, camera, video and photocopier, to enhance and supplement primary school art lessons.

The wide use of compatible computer equipment in many homes today ensures that many children are familiar with its use. Most classroom teachers recognise the valuable contribution 'information technology' (IT) can make to any art and design course by providing the children with the opportunity to work in a new and unique way using this fast developing medium.

Many of the children will already be familiar with the manipulation of screen images, sprite design and even colour mixing and printing. Some may even be downloading images from the Internet, editing the results and incorporating them into their own newsletter via desktop publishing. The view that the children should be entitled to access to IT in school is reinforced by the Revised National Curriculum Orders for Art (1995), which stipulates a requirement to provide opportunities for the children to apply and develop their IT capability in their study of art.

Computers and art in the classroom

The power of today's computers, together with their drawing, painting and design programmes, means that they are very effective tools for creative work.

Computers can be used to encourage the children to experiment freely with colours, shapes, textures and special effects. Images, either simple or complex, can be manipulated, altered, stored or repeated, while mistakes can be erased or altered with ease.

Software, including high quality shareware (free or low cost 'trial' software) for all of the computers found in schools is now readily available at low cost from many suppliers. Often, the purchase of a new computer includes 'bundled' software (several pieces of software sold as a package with the computer) suitable for classroom use.

A computer art module

An art module using a computer might involve:

- Drawing shapes on the screen using the mouse, either freehand or using the computer's pre-defined, inbuilt shapes or patterns.
- Filling the shapes with colour and/or texture using the software's fill or spray tools.
- Employing the cut-and-paste facility to restructure a design, perhaps using rotation and/or reversal of the image.
- Retaining the design for future use or development.
- Generating the design into a repeat pattern, again, using rotation or inversion.
- Printing out the design using a black and white printer or a colour inkjet printer on to paper, card or even fabric (using suitable inks and material).

Once techniques have been learned, computer-assisted design (CAD) can be further developed so that the children are able to produce patterns for specific purposes such as T-shirts or school notepaper.

CD ROM

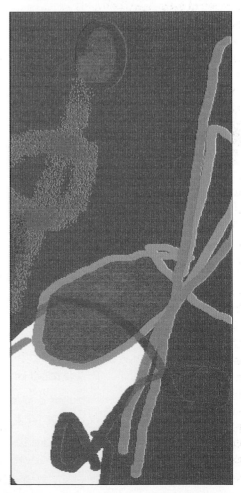

- Recent developments in IT hardware have resulted in high quality line definition and the availability of a wide variety of colours and patterns.

- The availability to primary schools of CD ROMs (computers that use CDs as discs), with their huge storage capacity, means that more complex but friendlier programmes are available. These programmes often come with as many as 2000 pre-drawn images, known as 'clip art', together with textures and patterns.

- But perhaps the greatest area of impact for the use of CD ROM is in art appreciation. CD ROMs containing hundreds of great works of art, which can be viewed sequentially as a slide show, are readily available.

- These images can also form part of a multi-media presentation and be examined closely whilst a sound track of information is played to the viewer.

- Similarly, the range of suitable software for art activities is expanding rapidly and teachers need to take every opportunity to trial packages and incorporate new material in their art scheme.

- For those teachers with little IT experience, a list of suitable basic software is included on page 61.

Safety

It is the responsibility of the class teacher to ensure a safe working environment for the children. A safety checklist should be incorporated in the Art Policy Document. Teachers should be encouraged to review the safety of the teaching environment regularly.

Safety checklist

- Are the children encouraged to develop an awareness of safe working practices?

- Do the children know what procedure to follow if an accident occurs?

- Is a first aid box readily accessible?

- Are safety notices clearly displayed?

- Is there a fire extinguisher and fire blanket available?

- Are the children aware of fire precautions that need to be taken?

- Do the children have access to protective clothing, such as aprons, goggles and gloves?

- Long hair can create dangerous situations and should be tied back.

- Is potentially hazardous equipment stored securely?

- Are containers clearly labelled?

- Glass bottles and jars should not be used.

- Are instructions about using materials and equipment followed rigorously?

- Do the children receive adequate supervision when using potentially dangerous tools and equipment?

- Is care taken to avoid excessive distribution of dust?

- Are kilns guarded correctly?

- Is the room adequately ventilated, especially when using aerosols and solvents?

- Do the children wash their hands after handling materials?

- Is food and drink prohibited during art lessons?

- Has a class routine been established for concluding practical activities?

- Is care taken to ensure that the classroom and equipment is properly cleaned after use?

Materials to support skills

Colour mixing

It is important that the children learn to mix colours from as young an age as three. They will then acquire the skills with which to paint creatively later.

To ensure that everyone is encouraged to mix colours NEVER buy orange, green, purple or brown.

Colours to buy

Red	Cerise
Cyan (blue)	White
Yellow	Black

And, if possible, as additional choices: crimson, Prussian blue and yellow ochre

Mixing

Do not worry if paint pots and palettes are not available; jar lids and yogurt pots are fine. Put a small amount of dry powder paint in a pot, two colours are enough to start (eg blue and yellow). White can be added as a third colour later.

Having experimented with two, then three colours, encourage the children to try four colours, for instance, blue, yellow, white and a red.

They could then try a different red (eg crimson) with black and yellow ochre.

Ideas for practising mixing colours

- Collect paint charts from DIY stores and let the children choose one to try and match.
- Create colour charts and invent names for the colours.
- Fold a piece of paper into six and fill each space with a different purple.
- Paint a blue stripe. Add a little white and paint another stripe. Repeat.
- Paint a blue stripe. Add a little black. Repeat as above.
- The children could mix a colour to match something they are wearing that day!

Easy method of mixing powder paint

Give each of the children a brush, a 'palette' and a pot of water. Then:

- wet the brush
- squeeze most of the water off the brush
- dip the brush in the dry powder paint
- take the brush to the palette
- mix the paint on the palette
- wash the brush between each colour
- it is important to talk the children through the process, stressing the importance of maintaining a consistency of mix (encourage them to add more powder or water to achieve this).

Using these skills

The children need to be experienced in colour mixing in order to gain confidence. It is also an important way of developing observational skills. Natural objects such as shells, rocks, fruit and vegetables, plants and flowers are ideal subjects. A structured approach to the skills involved will ensure that the children enjoy painting.

At first they don't need paper, the palette is enough.

Adding white and black are not the only ways to lighten or darken colours. Tones of colour can be achieved by, for instance, adding yellow to lighten green, or brown, purple or deep blue to darken a colour without 'deadening' it.

Pottery

The skills needed for pottery at KS1 and KS2 are associated both with techniques and equipment.

five basic techniques

Modelling – making a model or sculpture. For instance, modelling a basic shape and sculpting the shape by:
 – cutting
 – squeezing
 – applying clay (such as in free model making).

Thumb or pinch pot – making a thumb or pinch pot (straightforward pot made from circular or spherical shapes).

Slab pots

 – making tiles, or pots made from slabs of clay.

Coil pots

 – making coil pots (pots made using coils of clay on a clay base).

Decoration

 – decorating pots at both the initial making stage and at the glazing stage.

Pottery skills

The skills are also both practical (for instance, pottery demands skills in making and building techniques) and conceptual (for instance, it is necessary to have some knowledge about making pottery because there are rules which *must* be followed).

Technique	Practical Skills What children should be able to do	Conceptual Skills What children should know
MODELLING	☝ General modelling skills (forming a model from a lump of clay). ☝ Joining skills (using slip). ☝ Hollowing out a solid model using a spoon or hollowing tool.	☝ Know that clay is not like Plasticine. ☝ Know that if slip is not used the clay will not stay joined. ☝ Know that if a model is too thick it may blow in the kiln on firing.
THUMB OR PINCH POTS	☝ Pressing thumb or finger to right depth. ☝ Working the pot in the hand to make a round pot into a splayed out one. ☝ Getting it the right thickness. ☝ Joining pots with slip to make spherical shapes.	☝ Know that clay dries out if handled for too long. ☝ Know that slip must be used to join clay parts. ☝ Know that if two pots are joined together, then a hole must be made to let air out, or the pot will blow in the kiln.
SLAB POTS	☝ Rolling – between two guides; on stiff paper or cloth; roll from the middle of a flattened ball of clay. ☝ Cutting skills, should be decisive not hesitant. ☝ Pierce and smooth out any air bubbles. ☝ Joining slabs with slip. ☝ Forming clay round a cylinder to make cylindrical pots, with or without a base.	☝ Know that clay must not be rolled on smooth, highly polished surfaces or it will stick. ☝ Know that if air bubbles come up in a slab they must be burst, or the clay will blow in the kiln. ☝ Know that slip must be used to join clay.
COIL POTS	☝ Rolling coils to any even bore. ☝ Actual building skills, such as winding coils; joining coils with slip and smoothing coils for the outside of a pot.	☝ Know that slip must be used to join clay.
DECORATION	☝ Indented decoration: – pressing design in wet clay – scratching wet clay – carving leather-hard clay with a line cutting tool.	☝ Know that glaze will obscure any fine scratches.
Applied	☝ Applying clay shapes to surface: – use of slip/scoring two surfaces – mixing slips.	☝ Know that clay must be joined with slip. ☝ Know that slip is a mixture of clay and water.
Cutting out shapes	☝ Skill in using a corked needle to cut shapes out of slab pots or tiles.	
Glazing	☝ Use of brush on glazes (how to apply it and how many coats to use).	☝ Know that glaze sticks to anything it touches in the kiln. ☝ Know that bottoms of pots must not be glazed.

Progression of pottery skills

Key Stage 1

- Modelling

- Rolling for tiles

- Single thumb or pinch pots

- All decoration skills

- Coil pots in Year 2

Key Stage 2

- Advanced modelling and sculpting.

- Rolling for tiles – Year 3 and Year 4.

- Rolling slabs for cylinder-type pots – Year 5 and Year 6.

- Advanced thumb or pinch pots (with bases, fluted edges) – Year 3.

- Single joining of thumb pots – Year 4.

- Advanced joining of thumb pots to make animals, heads and so on – Year 5 and Year 6.

- Coil pots with more form and decoration.

- All decoration skills.

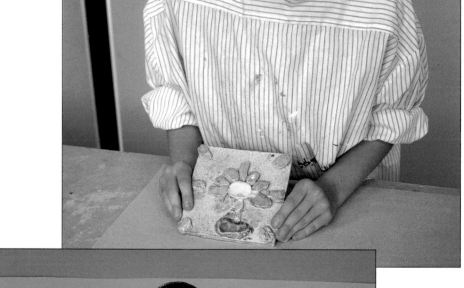

Conceptual skills

The children should be monitored by the teacher for those conceptual skills outlined for Key Stage 1.

The children at Key Stage 2 should have the relevant conceptual skills stressed to them and they should learn them.

A PRIMARY TEACHER'S HANDBOOK – *Art* © Folens

Basic equipment

Tables – the surface of tables should be covered with cloth or paper/plastic sheet.

Bins – plastic containers with lids or polythene bags (bin liners are useful for storage of clay) – check for holes. When clay is delivered check for holes in the plastic bag and re-tie the bag tightly with string. If storing for any length of time put the bags in a bin and cover them with damp sacking.

Plastic bags of various sizes – for storing unfinished work.

Aprons or shirts – roll up sleeves.

Wooden rolling pins and **rolling guides.**

Paper towels or **pieces of cloth** – for rolling clay on. (Not newspaper as this is too thin and will rip when the clay is being rolled.)

Modelling boards – covered with paper towels, used for placing pots on.

Hardboard or **plywood** – cut to size is ideal.

Cutting knives – NOT sharp Stanley knives. Old table knives are ideal and can easily be obtained from any junk shop or the school canteen.

Needles and **corks** – handy for cutting out detailed shapes. (Cork is used as a handle for the needle.)

Modelling tools.

Cutting wire – for slicing clay.

Rubber kidneys – kidney-shaped pieces of rubber used for smoothing clay.

Tools for decoration – nuts, bolts, screws, plastic and metal cylinders, pencils, combs, keys and hacksaw blades.

Two sets of squirrel hair brushes – one for slip, one for glaze.

Container of slip – clay mixed with water used for joining. (For safety reasons, do not use glass jars.)

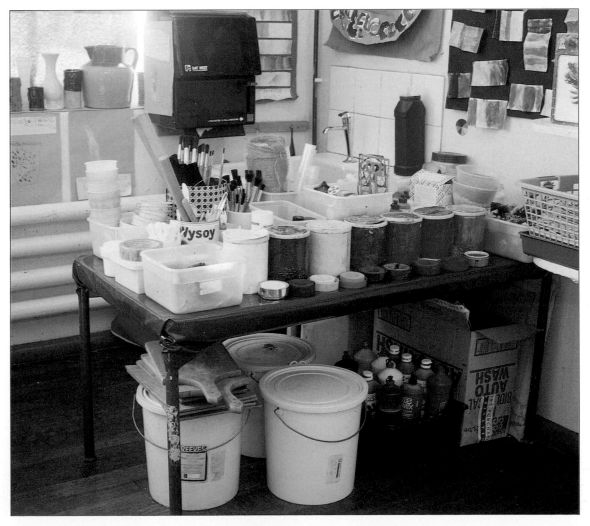

A selection of influential artists

The work of certain artists is particularly useful as a stimulus for studying the elements of art. Teachers may find the following information about artists helpful when planning lessons.

Artists concentrating on:

Tone and colour:

Rembrandt	Seventeenth century Dutch	Religious and allegorical paintings and etchings with an inner light.
Manet	Nineteenth century French	Portrait and interior paintings, pre-impressionist.
Pollock	Twentieth century American	Action painter. Disturbed surfaces rich in application.

Composition:

Michelangelo	Fifteenth century Italian	Paintings of religious figures.
Edgar Degas	Nineteenth century French	Dancers and interior paintings.
Stanley Spencer	Twentieth century British	Figurative works with unusual viewpoints, many religious in nature.

Above left: Salvador Dali's La Spectre et le Fantome. *Dali was famous for his surreal landscapes and figures.*

Expression:

Vincent Van Gogh	Nineteenth century Dutch	Figure and landscape painter with rhythm and movement.
Marc Chagall	Twentieth century Russian/French	Figure and landscape painter; romantic visions.
Salvador Dali	Twentieth century Spanish	Surrealist painter of figures and landscapes.

Colour:

Claude Monet	Nineteenth/twentieth century French	Garden and pond paintings (Impressionism).
Kandinsky	Twentieth century Russian	Abstract works, organic and geometric.
Rothko	Twentieth century American	Colour field (abstract) paintings.
Roy Lichtenstein	Twentieth century American	'Pop' art comic book, imaginary, large-scale works.

Below: Impressionist Claude Monet's Pond with Waterlilies, *painted in 1904.*

Line and movement:

Picasso	Twentieth century Spanish	Sculptures, paintings and drawings.
Matisse	Twentieth century French	Painter, draughtsman, collagist.
Bridget Riley	Twentieth century British	Op art painter non-figurative.

Form and shape:

Donatello	Fifteenth century Italian	Figurative sculpture – heroic subjects.
Paul Cézanne	Nineteenth century French	Landscape, still life and figure paintings.
Auguste Rodin	Nineteenth/twentieth century French	Robust figurative works.
Henry Moore	Twentieth century British	Figure and abstract works in the landscape.

Gustav Klint is famous for his patterned figurine works. Above is Fulfillment.

Paul Cézanne was a master of landscape, still life and figure paintings. Above, is his Boy in a red waistcoat.

Space and perspective:

Giotto	Thirteenth/fourteenth century Italian	Religious frescoes.
David Hockney	Twentieth century British	Interiors and American pools.

Atmosphere and light:

Joseph Turner	Nineteenth century British	Expressively painted landscapes – highly coloured.
Paul Nash	Twentieth century British	Surreal landscapes in a subdued palette.

Decoration – pattern:

Henri Matisse	Twentieth century French	Figurative interiors and gardens.
Gustav Klimt	Twentieth century Austrian	Patterned figure works.
Paul Klee	Twentieth century Swiss	Flat pattern in a subdued palette.

Minimum range of art materials

The following selection is a recommended list only. It is not exhaustive.

Paper
newsprint
tempera
cartridge
sugar
crêpe
gummed
poster
cellophane
card – thick, thin
and textured

Pencils
coloured
aqua
different grades
(from 4H to 4B)
charcoal

Textiles
fabrics
threads
haberdashery
weaving materials
dyes
fabric crayons
screens – squeegees

3D
clay (plus glazes,
slip, specialist tools)
impregnated
bandage
plaster of Paris
modelling clay
soap

Chalk
all colours

Charcoal
various thicknesses

Paint
powder
ready-mixed
acrylic
water colour

Applicators
brushes
straws
sponges
sprays
sticks
Lego
hands, feet

Adhesives
pva
glue sticks
cellulose powder
Blu-Tack
adhesive tape
cow gum
double-sided tape

Printing
blocks (polystyrene,
lino)
rollers
trays
cutters

Pens
felt tipped
italic
ball point

Crayons
thin
thick
printing

Inks
liquid
powder
printing

Pastels
greyhound
(ordinary)
oil
aqua

Recommended suppliers

Berol
Oldmedow Road, King's Lynn,
Norfolk PE30 4JR.

Daler–Rowney
Southern Industrial Area,
PO Box 10, Bracknell, Berkshire
RG12 8ST.

Specialist Crafts Ltd
(Reeves Dryad)
PO Box 247,
Leicester LE1 9QS

Esmond Hellerman Ltd
Hellerman House, Harris Way,
Windmill Road, Sunbury-on-
Thames TW16 7EW.

**Nottingham Educational
Supplies**
17 Ludlow Hill Road,
West Bridgford, Nottingham
NG2 6HD.

Acco Rexel Ltd
Gatehouse Road, Aylesbury,
Bucks HP19 3DT.

Yorkshire Purchasing
41 Industrial Park, Wakefield
WF2 0KE.

Philip and Tacey Ltd
Northway, Andover,
Hampshire SP10 5BA.

**POTTERY
Seawhite**
Star Road Trading Estate,
Partridge Green, Sussex RH3 8RA.

Pottery Crafts Ltd
Campbell Road, Stoke-on-Trent
ST4 4ET.

Kilncare Ltd
30 Norbury Avenue, Milton,
Stoke-on-Trent ST2 7BJ.

Useful resources

Books

Children's Growth Through Creative Experience, Art and Craft Education 8–13
Schools Council.
ISBN 0-442-29999-4.

Look Out! ILEA
(four booklets and three videos).

Art in Practice – Motivation and Development 3–12 Years
Margaret Morgan
(Nash Publishing
ISBN 1-898255-00-8).

Understanding Modern Art
(Usborne ISBN 0-7460-0475-3).

Teaching Art to Young Children 4–9)
Rob Barnes (Unwin Hyman
ISBN 0-04-371097-2).

An Eye on the Environment
H B Joicey
(Unwin Hyman
ISBN 0-7135-2622X).

Computer software

First Paint
Supplier: Keyboard Technology, The Resource Centre, 51 High Street, Kegworth, Derby DE74 2DA.

Pro Artisan–2
Supplier: Clares, 98 Middlewich Road, Northwich, Cheshire CW9 7DA.

Sketch
Supplier: Blackcat Software, The Barn, Cwm Camlais, Brecon, Powys LD3 8TD.

folens resource packs

The Folens series called *Art Packs* has been specially designed to help busy teachers link the exciting and creative practical aspects of art with the more theoretical and historical aspects.

In each pack, practical classroom art is developed through a close examination and awareness of significant works of art in a variety of media.

Each pack contains:
● 12 full-colour photographs of works of art – paintings, sculptures, ceramics, textiles etc
● two pages of miniatures of the photographs
● a 32-page Teacher Book containing information on the works of art, suggestions for pupil research, practical classroom activities based around the featured works of art plus a wealth of opportunities for pupil extension work in a variety of media.

The series comprises a variety of Art Resource Packs.
At Key Stage 1:
Influential Artists, Modern Artists and Art of Different Cultures.
At Key Stage 2:
Influential Artists, Modern Artists and Art of Different Cultures, Art of Ancient Civilisations and Art of the Tudors and Stuarts.
Suitable for both Key Stages:
Women Artists, Children in Art, Portraits and Victorian Artists.

Revelation Image Pro
Supplier: Longman Logotron, 124 Cambridge Science Park, Milton Road, Cambridge CB4 4ZS.

Colour Magic
Supplier: Research Machines, New Mill House, 183 Milton Park, Abingdon OX14 4SE.

Periodicals

Art and Craft
Scholastic Publications Ltd, CV1034, Westfield Road, Southam, Leamington Spa, Warwickshire CV33 0BR.

The Artist's and Illustrator's Magazine
Level 4, Fitzpatrick Building, 188-194 York Way, London N7 9QR.

Glossary of terminology

Abstract art
Non-representational art, that is, art that does not attempt to represent nature or recognisable subject matter.

Aesthetics
The philosophy of understanding and appreciation.

Appliqué
In embroidery, a fabric decoration (usually a pattern or picture) applied to fabric.

Armature
The framework or skeleton used by a sculptor as a base for modelling clay, plaster or impregnated bandage.

Avant-garde
Artists who innovate; styles, approaches and techniques far ahead of what is generally accepted.

Batik
A process of printing fabric, where the parts not to be dyed are covered by wax.

Cartoon
A full-size sketch ready to be transferred to canvas, a wall or tapestry. Traditionally, the drawing had holes pricked along the lines and was then 'pounced' through the holes with a bag of charcoal or chalk so that the design transferred.

The cartoon for Leonardo da Vinci's *Virgin and Child with St Anne* 1510–12 is in the National Gallery, London.

Classical
Usually art that is either Greek or Roman, or influenced by those styles.

Collage
A French term for describing artwork made up of materials stuck on to paper or canvas.

Colour
Colour has three main characteristics: hue, saturation or intensity, and tone or value. The hue is the name given to the colour (for example, red); saturation or intensity is the amount of pure hue (for example, a low saturation of red would produce pink); tone or value is the percentage of light in the colour (for example, pink has more light value than red).

Composition
Composition is the arrangement of colour, shape, line and so on in a picture, design or 3D shape.

Cubism
A movement in painting that abandoned traditional methods of modelling and perspective and portrayed a subject from several viewpoints at the same time.

Cubism was influenced by African sculpture and began with Georges Braque and Pablo Picasso.

Elements of art
A phrase much used in the National Curriculum for Art, it refers to the language of art. These are line, shape, tone, space, composition and colour.

Etching
A way of making a pattern or picture by engraving a metal plate with acids or corrosive substances, so that copies can be printed from it.

Expressionism
An artistic and literary movement that sought to express emotion through distortion and exaggeration of colour, shape, form and surface texture.

Formative influences were the late work of Vincent Van Gogh, Matisse and the Fauvists.

A PRIMARY TEACHER'S HANDBOOK – *Art*

Fauvism
Painting that uses colour to express emotion rather than reality. The Fauvists worked in the early twentieth century to free paintings from pictorial representation.

Figurative
Depicts recognisable people, animals or objects. The opposite of abstract art.

Fine art
Collective term to describe painting, sculpture, drawing and printmaking. The main difference between fine and applied or decorative art is that fine art serves no practical purpose.

Folk art
Objects and decoration made by people without formal training who use traditional techniques and forms. Objects are usually handmade, lively and colourful.

Form
The artist's way of seeing and the artist's way of presenting that way of seeing.

Fresco
Colour applied to a wall covered in wet plaster so that the finished painting is 'fresh' and dries to become part of the wall.

Futurism
Italian movement at its height from 1909–14 which attempted to capture the beauty of speed and the machine.

Genre
A French term meaning 'variety' applied to paintings about everyday domestic life, also meaning category or type of painting.

Impressionism
An art movement significant to nineteenth century European art

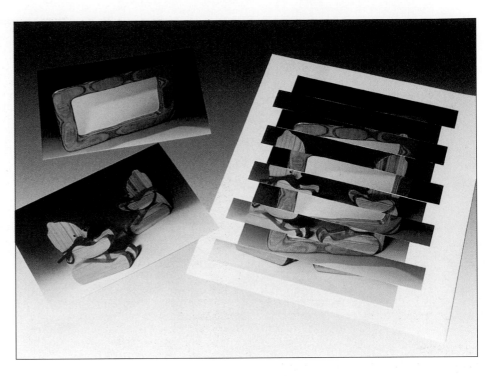

taking its name from Claude Monet's painting *Impression ... Sunrise*. Impressionists captured the effects of light and atmosphere by working in broken brushstrokes with bright colours on a white ground. They were the avant-garde artists of their time.

Landscape
Can be a subject in its own right, or provide a backdrop for another subject.

Line
Lines create form and shape, both inside and around the edge of a shape. They can be thick, thin, curved, straight, long, short or broken.

They can be expressive, creating mood in a drawing or painting.

Lithography
A process of obtaining prints from an inked metal or stone surface that has been treated so that the areas to be printed are ink-receptive and those not to be printed are ink-repellent.

Monochrome
Tones of single colour; or a painting or print made in one colour only.

Montage
Selection, cutting and piecing together of photographs.

Neo-impressionism
A development of impressionism where painters used the latest colour theories in a planned and scientific manner. They used lots of colours close together so that, from a distance, they merged.

Georges Seurat was the greatest painter of this movement.

Op art
Developed in the 1960s. Paintings that used colour and pattern to create an optical illusion, often to create the impression of movement.

Bridget Riley is one of its best known exponents.

Perspective
Developed in the thirteenth century as a way of making a 2D surface look 3D.

Photogram
Simple photograph produced without using a camera. An object is placed on photographic paper, exposed to light and the paper developed. (The process needs to be carried out in a dark-room.)

Pigment
Colouring agent that determines the final colour of a paint or dye.

Pin-hole camera
a simple camera made from a small box containing a small pin hole that admits light on to light-sensitive film.

Pop art
An art movement which was at its peak in the 1960s. The artists took images from the consumer society and popular culture such as television, comics and advertisements as a basis for their work. They also used commercial methods of production, such as printing.

Best known artists are David Hockney, Roy Lichtenstein and Andy Warhol.

Renaissance
The revival of classical style art and architecture in between the fourteenth and sixteenth centuries. It started in Italy and spread throughout Europe.

Famous artists include Michelangelo, Raphael, Botticelli, Leonardo da Vinci.

Romanticism
An eighteenth century movement that reflected the mood of the time, stressing the emotional aspect of artworks, often including some horror or mystery. Scenes from literature, struggles with the elements and nostalgic ruins were themes.

Famous artists include Turner, Dalacroix and Géricault.

Shape
The depth of an object as opposed to a flat, 2D picture. An illusion of space on flat surfaces can be made by using perspective.

Slip
A mixture of clay and water used to help bond two pieces of clay.

Sprite
A design composed of small, coloured squares that can be moved with great speed and accuracy on the computer screen.

Surrealism
This movement is concerned with the subconscious and dreams. Surrealism is much influenced by the work of Sigmund Freud.

Best known artists are Salvador Dali and Joan Miró.

Tapestry
Thick, hand-woven textile fabric often used as wall hanging.

Texture
Representation in a work of different surfaces.

Tint
A change in a colour when a small amount of a different colour is added.

Tone
The amount of dark and light in a colour, for example, red becoming pink when white is added.

Vanishing point
The point or points at which parallel lines appear to meet on the horizon line.

Wash
Paint or ink diluted to produce a thin, transparent layer that can be put on as a wash over broad areas.